More Praise for *Wild Pack of the Living*

Grief and beauty, art and compassion inform this extraordinary collection which has at its core a sequence based on the abduction of Steven Stayner at seven years old. The poems are rendered in diction stark in its power, yet they also speak in the most delicate and poignant imagery. For example, remembering her own forced separation from her mother, the speaker says of herself and Steven, "after this happened/ the rain on a leaf/ no longer belonged to either of us." Cleary's exploration of loss and separation continues in the sections "Jane Doe" and "Hospice Rounds" in language simultaneously accurate and unexpected. Luminous and empathetic but never sentimental, this collection is a gift of hope and clarity from an exceptional talent. Cleary has put her considerable poetic gifts and generous spirit into poems that never prettify but elevate and redeem the human condition.
—**Kathleen Aguero**, author of *World Happiness Index*

WILD PACK OF THE LIVING

EILEEN CLEARY

Nixes Mate Books
Allston, Massachusetts

Library of Congress Control Number: 2023949565

ISBN 978-1-949279-51-1

Nixes Mate Books
POBox 1179
Allston, MA 02134
nixesmate.pub

for all children forcibly separated from their loving families

Dear Reader,

When I was a teenager, Steven Stayner, who had been abducted from his family and who had gone missing for seven years, escaped his captor and returned home, freeing a second boy, Timothy White, in the process. To me, Steven was a hero because I had been seized from my family by the state, in what felt like a legally sanctioned abduction. My brother Carl also went missing (stolen by his foster family) and was lost to us for 40 years. My experience and Steven's are not identical. They are emotional cousins.

This book holds Steven Stayner – that boy from Merced who has lived in my chest for forty years. It also holds being among the missing. Once a child has been forcibly removed from their home and family, and has been assigned a new name and biography, there is no going back to being fully among the living.

CONTENTS

JANE DOE

HOSPICE ROUNDS

WILD PACK OF THE LIVING

1 : BOY FROM MERCED

I'd stop seeing the parkway where Red Ball Gas persists
long after it closed for business. The service clerk
sponging the windshield, dusty as a country road,
could finally retire. If I recognized Stevie, sluggish
in the backseat, I'd see where the sedan's spectacled driver –
nearly hairless, hyperglycemic, haphazardly eluding
capture – must be fleeing. And I'd pursue him,
learning by heart his license plate and face.
The hard years of his years. His wintering.
I'd rid his Buick's trunk of its church fliers with fake monks,
shred the ruse he printed to appeal to the gullible
and plain-old religious, every one with a young son.
I'd gag his *Give to the poor, Mrs. Jones and Mr. Bean* –
He's out of Grimm's, with sleeping pills spilled
in the console, coursing through Yosemite.

If he leaves no tracks on the packed ground of Tioga Pass,
who can follow where he crossed into the camp. I can't
think because of the cabin I'd be forced to tour.
I might have to touch.

      not a monster, per se –

more like eyes torching dry leaves in fire season.

BEYOND THE TIRE SWING AND TOY BOATS,

amongst tossed bottles,
plastic bags,
cans rusted and a sparrow dead,
this hill shoulders the sky.

If a child doodled these clouds,
he wouldn't call them swollen.

To cry while squirrels crook
the trees would be absurd.

Cruel, my heart reminds me
that once a boy was stolen
from his home and that

no one could find him;
it whispers, *you were taken too.*

Or, is the word *taken* too strong?
I was removed.

Let me say this:

after this happened
the rain on a leaf
no longer belonged to either of us.

DEAR GRIEF-LAKE,

We failed to notice you circling
our gates in the denning season.

You breached the park, Dear Predator,
where we latched our children between
crisp grass and wooly clouds,

scraped the soil,
showered your scent
across the playyard,

Dear Raptor. Dear Innocence Eater,
Slash Monger, Star Stealer,

you approached in the way we
tried to seal you out, telltale
blue smoke of your breath

vanishing. How happy we were,
blind and unaware of you crouched there.

Parnell smothers every flower he encounters.
In this way, seaside daisies, cliff maids,
and their silhouettes wane
under his two-bit clouds. They break
away from him like branches deprived of sun.
He's a carnie moving in on his target
like warm air drenched in funnel cake.

To help snatch the boy,
Parnell chooses Murph, a slow bloke
who miscounts coins in life's sweaty line for cotton candy.
Murph pays no never mind to the smell of vomit,
or the shrieking for the ride to stop.

Parnell grooms Murph so that on the right day,
say Decemeber 4, 1972
they cram his Buick with Christian pamphlets
and creep through the oaks
on Yosemite Parkway, hunting for Big Wheels,
            Radio Flyers,
                  and their freshly minted drivers.

ABDUCTION : abdūcere "to lead away"

A grimy white car pulls Stevie's eyes from his feet.

abdūctiōn-, abdūctiō "allurement."

Parnell drives. Murph invites. Stevie climbs

inside.

Capture the Flag. Leapfrog. Walked Back for Backpack. Freeze Tag.
Kick the Can. Captured Flag. Haystack. Four Winged Beetles. Sewing
Needles. Swing. DoubleDutch. Empty Slingshot. Re-load. Puddle
Jumps. Croaking Toad. Skipping Stones. Shoelace Loose. Bike Race.
Flat Tire. Chain Broken. Red Rover. Duck Duck Goose. Keep Away.
Treasure Hunt. 7-Up. Sidewalk Chalk. Cops and Robbers. Found
Quarter. Kick Ball. Leaf Pile. Late Fall. Baseball. Giant Step. Ant Hill.
Fire Drill. Friend's House. Stickball. Puppy Found. Lost Shoe. Slinky.
Merry-go-round.Hopscotch. Skipping Rope. Thumb Wrestle. Red
Light. Waiting for the Streetlight. Cat's Cradle. Penny Toss. Hide 'n
Seek. Simon Says. Four Square. Truth of Dare. Candy Store. Mother
May I. Five Minutes More.

undetected, except
by the smooth-haired terrier.

    Not the same pet who trailed the Boy Scouts,
    while they searched the Parkway's
    empty lots and gas stops
    before the soggy cold drove
    them inside. And not the junkyard
    dog, wary of flashlights in the tall weeds,
    who sniffed the frightened hands that pried
    open scores of refrigerator's doors.

As far as anyone can tell,
Parnell stripped the boy and dyed his hair,

By cabin windows black oaks sought the light.

Dog lilies and the lark spurs may have heard,

       Your parents don't want, don't need, can't feed

What it was like to morning into the valley of forget-me-not.
Not waking from sleep so much as into a chasm,

the hours weathering clefts in their spleens, streams
carving them wide – their boy calling
along the trailhead. Muffled, distant –
through packed shovels of doubt.

For a brief time, any wind could have been him
rising from his bunk into rockfall,
with no ladder from which to return.

The eggs uncracked on the counter,
coffee gone cold.

NAME: Steven Gregory Stayner. Song before "Time for supper." Or "Wait till your father."

FROM: Merced, California. Mrs. Walsh's second grade. The orchard where Daisy fetches sticks.

DATE: December 4, 1972 and every day since.

AGE: 7. We like to think that his bones lengthen, muscles strengthen and birthdays make him older every year.

EYES: Brown. Shade of fawn or baby bear, a walking stick, or a baseball mitt.

HAIR: Shag. Combed on tiptoes in front of the mirror.

SCARS: None. That we know.

COMPLEXION: Fair and freckled.

CLOTHING: Never found.

When the abductee's mother overhears
– *one less mouth to feed* –

the words puncture her tissue paper chest,

pummel the chambers beneath,
beat them into a bird.

Even in April Kay knows
the grove is snowing almonds,

and that the bees are dancing
to direct the lost back to their hives.

If only she could breathe,
she could fill her lungs with spring.

It hadn't rained.
They'd driven from school instead.

His brother met him on the parkway,
and his father wasn't sick in bed.

It had been any other Monday
and mother hadn't run out to buy bread.

They don't preserve his crayon
on the garage door
or any place he scribbles to tell
the house, "My is name is Steven" or
"I like to draw" and "I can spell."

They never have to know their Stevie's name
was changed to Dennis Gregory Parnell.

THE PEACH CANNER TO HIS MISSING SON

after Paul Nemser

Long past these peach trees,
                the innocent hour tills.

The orchard's arms open, as if expecting
                to surround you, child.

Time is a hummingbird I can't outdistance,
                secreted on a fragile limb.

A curve of blossoms overhead, and blossoms heavenward
                petal this narrow prayer.

An orchard in which I concede you're missing
                and orchards in which I still miss you.

Orchards bent-double with frost.
Globes glimmer   ablaze,   as is their way.
Sapwood chants Restore the sun.

Rows pivoted green by the earth,
                rows blushed pink by a meadow-birthing star.
The pearl at the center lingers, snow-melt slaking its thirst.

I am calling you back to the orchard, the orchard I must
one day abandon.

This grove forfeits a measure of heat
each time your little shadow sends no word.

and Apollo, NASA's J-crew,
    heard night after day, and each afternoon, that
he still wasn't home from school. They almost spied
    him at a greasy spoon, and knew before Bear Creek
was dragged that Stevie hadn't sank. God planted
    a man inside every boy, so he might reach
his height. If Stevie were with them,
    he would jump higher, throw a ball six times
farther. Is he buried in the peach fields?
    He could be among their blossoms. Call him.
He might lie among the plums, the almonds,
    or the dunes. If he were with Cernan,
Schmitt or Evans, he'd trail a pathfinder,
    rejoin Merced's atmosphere, land safely
from the moon. Our hero would be home.

SUN GHAZAL WITH BURNT OUT SHERS

after Dorianne Laux

Red in the face the first time I faced it. The sun,
hanging since before the first someone, the sun

dipping amber fingers into dewy-cool lawns.
A warming cabinet for grass blankets, the sun,

call it day-star. Luminous over hayfields, loosed
in the furs of chipmunk. Honey: homespun sun,

a taffeta dress stitched with lemon zest, rested
in an ocean blue backdrop. Dear Sun,

Like a frantic greenhouse, I've a blind spot when
it comes to what's too hot, Smothering One,

I love you like a child though you scorch me.
O Variant of Helen, for what's left of eternity.

IN WHICH STEVIE'S GRANDFATHER UNWITTINGLY
LIVES IN A TRAILER PARK 200 FEET FROM
THE CABIN WHERE STEVIE'S HELD

This was before his captor enrolled him in Steele Lane Elementary
where Kay and Del had mailed missing person bulletins

which never made it to his classroom. The Little Red Cabins
were tucked behind Judy's Trailer Park, so the captor and Stevie's

grandfather pulled their trucks in the shared access road.
The same road police passed but never searched

on their way to Yosemite, where they searched but never looked
for Kenneth Parnell, because his name escaped the personnel

list supplied by the desk clerk, who was not the same clerk
who trashed the police photos.

    This was before the boy was stripped lakeside,
                at the hands of a masked king.

    The incense burned and never reached the reeds.
                We couldn't see.

as a thought fills an empty space,
worry becomes a planet.

Great Circle in the Sky,
how did we get here?

Every time we push this cart,
this Earth pushes back.

So lonely. The tornado
implicates the butterfly.

A close up reveals
the boy on the roadside

after all, is a sapling,
and he was never waving.

RENAMING STEVEN GREGORY STAYNER

A rose by any other renders Stevie
an only, signals so long
the buck- toothed middle, his dog,
his bottle-green frame house
and patchwork lawn.

Steven, *like a merry voice meaning crown.*
Steven, meaning *loud call*, meaning *yell*,
skinned to its middle, its Greg, meaning *bell*.
No. Meaning *watchful*.

A Steven by any other senses
his given name's a wreath,
scribbles almond groves
on a garage door where his father weeps,
but refuses to wash away

As Stevie's captor sets up
shop to sell bibles or broken
TVs, his real dad stops
fishing at the lake and camping
with his kids near Bear Creek Bay.

The target moves whenever
a lawful neighbor smokes out
Kenneth Eugene Parnell.

Who can say what a boy hides
between stones in his pockets.

The barred owl's baritone gives way
to the tiny engine of morning cicadas
in Del's village of grieving, waking
his rooms truer than steamed coffee
filtering the black and white photograph
of his boy in Wranglers and cowboy boots
outside of Charles Wright Elementary.

Door of an ear against a cool sheet.
There might as well be asters in his
feet. How long? What is soon
but a country with open borders:

impossible to know who will pass through.
Or when. For now, a cardinal trills life- life.
Soon the wind through honeysuckle,
hornets shying outside their paper nests
next to a ladder set out since yesterday's rain.

THIRTEEN REASONS STEVIE'S SEVEN YEARS LATE FROM SCHOOL

I

Missing child posters
trashed.

II

Fireflies do not answer
when lightning bugs are called.

III

Hidden in the open city.
Who am I?

IV

Father and son
Act 1
New father; same son.
Act done.

V

We know to search for
a gunny sack in a ditch.
but not a boy at a school desk,
not a boy at recess.

VI

The grimy window's a veiled lens.
Half-hidden by fern.
The cabin's peeling dove-grey.

VII

O most trusted man in America,
Why is this news too old?
Mr. Cronkite, Don't you see
how Stevie outgrows his shoes?

VIII

Giving a Manchester Terrier
tied the boy to him.

IX

He washes and rinses the boy's mind,
leaves it blowing on the line.

X

Though neighbors noticed his strange,
Parnell not meeting their eyes,
his tight lips about the boy,
they never made an outcry.

XI

Parnell drove to work each night
in a gasping Buick
certain
that the silhouette of his threats
would hold.

XII

Though Steven's heart flutters,
it doesn't flee.

XIII

He was seven for seven years.
the perverse was getting worse.
Still the boy tarried,
trapped between Mendocino and Merced.

after Elizabeth Bishop

Don't think of unbroken mustangs in the sagebrush
rounded up like gangsters, their captive gallopings.

Don't think of helicopters startling them
into holding pens. How one mare fractured
in the frenzy, how the others ears stung

when they'd heard the shot. Don't think about
the orphaned foals whose hoofs don't recall
grassy loam or their mother's grooming,

not ghost lullabies nickered in distant trees,
or the maples held helpless in any act
of resisting the herd's capture.

How once strong legs thundered
through prairie rocks and wild roses.

The awkward 7th grade, all arms and legs,
voices soaring & falling, finally cracking.

Guitar strings stretched too tight. Steven frets
under fluorescence, where he reads with the others

an article on lost children. This isn't that wildlife
magazine where he learned to track backyard

animals whose prints vanish when mud meets grass cover.
A good ranger looks for clues: a trunk where a buck rubbed its antlers,

baby squirrels susurring oak leaves, a hollow where a red fox sleeps.
Junior Scholastic says to solve a mystery, be curious.

Today brings Steven as close as he's ever been to telling.
How strange the words feel, a fat pigeon's feathers coughed

from his throat. He chokes, *I miss my family*, though
no one hears. The teacher doesn't mean to brush him aside,

it's just that the recess bell rings, and the class clamors to play outside.

PARNELL ABDUCTS A SECOND CHILD FEBRUARY 13, 1980

Meet your new brother – Kenneth Parnell to teenaged Steven Stayner

Timmy fidgets in the makeshift barber's chair,
his dye-stained T-shirt, a Rorschach.

He peeks past Parnell to the threshold
at Stevie, just back from school.

Stevie translates one inkblot:
Oh God! He took this kid!

Another warns, *this is not a test.*

The next blot's a boy
    Stevie could have been
or years ago he was.
       Steven as Timmy,
hair- dyed in the doorway
        reliving that first day,

    through the knots in his fingers.

An old wind breaches
the crack of a window painted shut,
   carries news from Stevie's first country:

       Stevie? *STEVEN.*
         Bring Timmy home.

We never gave you away.

           Stevie,

The sun's diplomats arrive
at the grimy windows
from cloudseas,
a million coral photons
pinging the glass,
heating it alive.

On the ground outside:
a beached rock
seacarved with a whale's face.
Its two-fielded eye tracks for tides,
not the only one
who contemplates a return.

ESCAPE

Steven straps a Bowie to his boot,
                won't go to school.
One Saturday when Parnell's at work
                Steven packs bologna
        and hitches a ride
                through redwoods on Highway 41,
        carrying Timmy on his back, "I got you."

        Past farms and groves. Peach trees
                        usher them,
                between the towns,
                "I got you."
        In Ukiah, blue lights disclose the boys.

        Hands deep in the pockets of his muddy Levi's
                the teen mumbles to police,

"I know my first name is Steven
                and this is Timmy White. I brought us home.
                        Is my real father alive?"

One day Shōichi Yokoi stitched civilian straight-line,
state sanctioned fall-collared jackets in National Defense Drab, under
the pagodas in Aichi Prefecture, and the next he'd landed in Guam,
slogging through fox grass, *never surrender* ringing in his spleen.
His platoon splintered, spreading men to defend themselves
as piteously as kingfishers hand-fed to tree snakes. The first news
that the war ended never reached Shōichi. For decades he foraged
wild nuts, mangos, shrimp, snails, venomous frogs,
and the occasional rat, then stowed them in his self-dug cave,
only slowing to erase his footprints in the undergrowth.
It may surprise you that when Shōichi was found,
he'd already known that his enemy had put down his gun.
He apologized: *a good son should never be captured alive.*
Thus he never left the hole he'd burrowed and lined with bamboo,
or the eel traps and hand-made looms so far from the rooms of his youth.

A digression of dirt
    sinks
    his days between seedling and ripe berry.

How murky Steven's account
    recorded to forget.

He spun within a godlike wholesomeness
    the divorce of before and after,
    unlooping a knot in the dark.

ABDUCTED BOY RETURNS HOME AFTER 7 YEARS – *NEW YORK TIMES* MARCH 4, 1980.

He couldn't have known how much
    his parents would shrink inside

their pea green frame house,
    or that his once small siblings

would outsize their twin mattresses,
    or that his first collie would be fenced

only in Before's invisible lawn.
    Now he can only speak of:

cow and pigs, the farm they still owned
    Before He Went Missing.

During's verboten.
    Sometimes, if he recalls During,

his brain projects that scene
    on the screen of his sweatshirt pulled

over his eyes so that his parents can't see
    that he did smile in the lost centuries.

His memory shows him smoking with friends
        in the woods, or rafting on a lake between two cliffs.

If he claps his hands he can measure
        the distance between Boy Then and Boy Now.

Never enough hands to cover his mouth
        if he dares to share anything blue:

blue geraniums outside a busted trailer,
        blue lupines, blue flax

or blue panic attacks.
        Sometimes, the night is blue-black,

and his mind maps
        the migration of the one whale

no one else can hear.
        Meanwhile

cicadas broadcast
        their secrets; they tymbal

their miniature drums,
        spreading their news

instead of hiding in their rooms
        or staying out late after school.

KEEPING UP APPEARANCES ON ABC NEWS
MARCH 14, 1980

Live from a Sacremento living room,
televised before the dawn birds bridged into chorus,
      about two weeks after his escape,
in an interview where Steven Stayner sports
      a coffee-colored jacket dwarfing his shoulders
as his parents flank either side of the couch,
Del wearing his beige leisure suit, and Kay
      decked in her browniest slacks and lemon sweater vest,
the reporter noting that off camera,
      a lawyer would make sure not to compromise
their abduction case, their son can't remember
      which days during his seven years held captive
he thought which thoughts, and Del admitted
      that he'd lost hope, which opposed
what the viewers were told in the lead-in,
      so the questions volley to Kay,
who dutifully chirps that she had gone *about my merry way*
      presumably unflummoxed, vacuuming and packing
school lunches for her other four.

CLOSURE

Say the child returns
seven years older, freckles gone.
Same child, same chromosomes
but he's outgrown his pants, his plastic comb.
He smiles politely. He's otherwise withdrawn.

The child who vanished curbside:
He's vigilant. Wary. Fire-eyed.
Or shall we say, sharkeyed,
fishing even asleep.

Dear Wrecked One, Dear Body of Evidence,
We are scrubbed at the table for your christening.

The salmon patch your mother called an angel kiss
blooms on the bridge of your nose.

Meanwhile, we'll drill any clue from you,
extract a missing tooth until your name escapes.
                    In Truth,
    we surmise. We theorize.
        And if the dead room answers,
    is it okay that we never asked
            what you thought,
                        (all this so your captor will be caught?)

    Dare we ask, if we could skip this last bit,
        and promise to tell no one,
    Would you rather we return you to your
    bed of blue chiffon and snowberries,

        that we kept your body
    from this strange and wild pack of the living –

REINCARNATION STORY: PARNELL
TRANSMIGRATES INTO A CORPSE PLANT

One day he's in his wheelchair
propositioning Diane who
delivers his liquid nutrition,
and pricing fake birth certificates
while bidding on local children.
Before you know it, he's in a prison
hospice, just thinking about
that stupid bitch ratting him out.
If she had just bought him
that kid, he'd be in his apartment
right now. Instead, four years later,
still wistful for what might have been,
he flatlines. Not long after,
the great sequoias,
each genus of orchid, and every species
of Yosemite's meadow grass,
that had for so long mutely stood
by the children he'd stolen
and smuggled onto their homeland,
exhale. In exquisite relief, the moon sickles,
and Parnell rebirths as *Amorphophallus Titanium*
As in prior life, Stevie's abductor
approximates human temperature. In the old body,

he stalked and trapped a new boy
nearly every seven years.

Now, he manifests solely as a wound.
O, Karma! O, Carrion!

BLUE-AND WHITE, 1989 KAWASAKI EX-500 PAID FOR WITH THE $30,000 FROM THE MINISERIES *I KNOW MY FIRST NAME IS STEVEN*

Because the couple couldn't agree
on whether dilled cucumber
blossoms should be coins or spears,
because two ends don't meet
between raking leaves
and tossing pizza dough,
Steven motored home in the rain
after another short estrangement.

Because his helmet was stolen
two months prior, because
a tired migrant-worker
pulled onto a puddled drive,
because it's hard to keep
two biographies alive
in one body,
Steven Gregory Stayner,
who once rescued himself
on air, died.

REINCARNATION STORY: BOY BECOMES MANCHESTER TERRIER

Ancestor of the Greyhound, he courses toward
an elusive windsock some would call a wish,
proving that not every animal who's lost has vanished.
Forget that even as this dog, his heart might rupture
in childhood. See him wheel for a fly ball and catch
the sun in a field of metalmarks and finches.

PORTRAIT OF MISSING CHILD AS A CLOUD

Caged by trees, could be a boy.
Another's hands stroking or strangling.
Or are these day moon ponderings?
Even if this is the child, he cannot answer.
So, do not ask: *is that you?*

You cannot reach him,
though he seems to stir in you.
And who is mute,
if you hear him whisper
and do not answer.

Because the sky grieves to hold him,
this parcel of air is heavy,
sultry and purple, pressed on the rangy
shoulders of wild saplings.

Years and the cloud has not disclosed
itself. Are you Nobody too?

II : JANE DOE

No one answers. She calls again. The throatless stars don't call back. How long has she been lying here? North of insomnia. South of sleep-walking. She's not dead. Not dead. She shuts the porch light off to discourage moths because their dusty wings distract her from thinking about Joubert's Clothing Store. How tomorrow she'd walk there and finally get to buy autumn outfits for the girls. She loves to poke around that shop. Sometimes she writes lists of designs she sees on the racks, and imagines which days of the week she'll dress her babies in them. Monday: tulle coveralls. Tuesday: skirted rompers. Someday: the heritage sweaters with matching cotton tights. If only Joubert's would offer a lay-away. Maybe she'll inquire tomorrow, she'd thought just before she never opened the screen door to go back in. She must try to stay awake, knows she must have lost consciousness and thinks: my girls are home alone. Or worse. They aren't. Whoever did this to me could have circled back for them. That is why she crawls to the roadside, which she would tell the officer. If only her mouth would work.

The hunter moon spills
over a gathering
of blue-men, blue-lit.

Janie, Mommy, Aunty J, age unknown of Some Town.
Born: under a Barley Moon. Died: after the thrash
without her family by her side. Daughter of the sky,
she was raised near a spruce, and all of its noble blue.
Jane was a mentor for a crop of friends, who recall
her as "that girl we used to know." Girl we should call.
Her last dollar? She'd rather give it than have it stolen.
Janie believed in forgiveness. She once costumed
a dog in a unicorn horn, and we hope that pet escaped.
She was occasionally missed before she vanished.
Survivors include her son, nieces, nephews, and their
grown-ups. She's preceded in death by the summer,
and a lover. In lieu of flowers, send her home.

III : Hospice Rounds

FOR MY BROTHER JOHNNY AT 61

After Dorianne Laux

A quick sign of the cross for the boy in the cowboy hat,
dimpled and smiling as if this blessing could mean a pulsing
rope never squeezed his neck for too many newborn minutes,
as if he might not jump off the roof once he's no longer
content to belt out *Delta Dawn* and *What's Going On*
with a transistor radio in his lap, long after the 9 Volt dies.
As if the staff at yet another group home would never lecture
that Johnny is a man and because he is a a man
we no longer can bring him plastic replicas of Barney Rubble
munching cocoa pebbles from a clay bowl, even though
we know Barney as a noble-hearted man who loves
his feral boy, though that boy misuses his strength, though
others might leave him to be raised by wild mastodons.

Death too early? Little death in me. She, ill: prepared.
Two more days, three at best. Still. I wanted. But she left,
soundlessly, a bell unstruck in my heart's greensward,
The wind confusing the grass. *Who goes there?* A field
as if Wyeth's Christina never crawled its pasture.
Body refusing its presence. She had to be hand fed.
What's the consensus? *For you were not hungry and I*
Did not feed. The grains assembling into uneaten. All
that threshing and winnowing for not. Spent toast.
The small tiger unbagging itself; it was out all along.
She had already selected her velvet gown. Vigiling, we
were the last souls allowed, our past lives little folklores.
Never wanted a wheelchair, never sanctioned a narrow
saddle. Instead, blue wind. Air. A yawning door.

Outside my hospice office, two men I pronounced dead visit as crows
on telephone poles, their voices as soft as a morphine dose.
Parking lot pines don't mind returning as pines. Then, a third death.
A woman in a Murphy bed under a skylight. Her eyes don't absorb
this snapshot stars arranged two thousand years ago.
I think about the provinces the dead occupy,
especially my friend whom I did not pronounce, though I felt her

pulse wane while my ear pressed against her chest. I can't find her.
One crow is an old man. The second, younger man had my friend's eyes.
Now he's a crow in the space of a few hours. The sky's shedding its skin.
The woman waits for me to look for signs of life. This woman
hasn't let go of her living yet. I do this for her: stall.
Keep her family occupied. Give her time to leave. Tuesday morning
another pine carves a dark swan into its bark while six hawks lay bare the sky.

If instead he perches on his bed while
his grandson bolts through the room
toting a Mo Willems book and duck.
If chickadees *seet*. Or an owl speaks.
If pine warblers blur. If he won't stir
to watch the birdbath from the corner
nook. If whippoorwill and still.
When it rains and petrichor doesn't lure
him to the pitch pines. If full count
in the ninth and the Red Sox need a hit.
If he lists. If he squints. Before you lean
and whisper, *Let go*. He'll send signals,
you'll know.

On Tuesday, he checks on the snapdragons,
and finds in his window planter
(how extravagant!) downy owlets
standing at attention like traffic cones
signaling a detour. Which is why John calls
his oncologist. *Somethings*, John says,

can't be predicted. Napping hatchings
should plummet to the ground but they
hang on by their back toes. John hangs up,
collects rocks and pebbles
to construct a border for his garden.

How gorgeous, the world.
His pancreas stabs him in his gut
right there with the owlets watching.
The snapdragons holding graceful
against the beating sun are the last
vivid things he remembers

before the dark hour visits upon his head.

What he recalls less clearly
in the anemic chill of that hour

is the porchlight
that must mean *home*.

These folks who crowd
this room look like his family,
(almost like, only they sob
when they speak of him.)

The person most resembling
his wife tells him to *go home*,
            but has no atlas.

                  Instead,
night spreads like butter on toast
he won't chew through,
until, right in front of these temporary
people he knows but does not know,
and to spite all of their feathered kindnesses,
his pancreas strikes again, hard.

John extends his arms above his head,
swings his legs out of bed, and launches.

The pinched hour unfastens its grip.
Wild fingers press into sedges and soft rush.
       Oh. See her.
Not in this bedroom, too bright,
her body too like itself to be denied,
but as a firefly across the lawn
       follow so long
to the invisible side of this lake.
Pack up her wires, her brushes. Set loose her tools.
Daylilies escort her to a trail already smoothed.

SELF-PORTRAIT OF HOSPICE NURSE ON THE ROAD WITH FALLEN POLE

& downed pines trap me.
Houses where no one can see
through the hazy air polluted

with ghosts and piped with grief,
those twin pixies out to ruin
what's left of peaceful nights.

Not snow but angels in pairs
dust the air, until they crowd
family conversations with God.

I haven't had time to let go
of the last visit,

find myself trying
to move a live wire, boots iced,
the patient's neighbor taking my hand,

I waited for you.

Who am I?
Hunted,
a hare shot by a fear it can't outrun.

It's a trick to fly over ice, hearing
what groans and creaks beneath.

The stars telescope to a living room
where I assure a partner,
he waited for you to step away.
Luckily, the night cottons its ears.
Near the foothills, a child sleeps
through banshee's cries. A gust
interrupts the pines. In another doorway
a halting voice calls, *I think.*
A second man unburdened.
By morning, grown children make
their way across first lawns.
Venus is best seen an hour before dawn.

They stare through bedroom windows.

Shortness of breath, a cough no longer
mattering so much.

I hardly know what to say.

They can say everything with a straight face.

Listening, Listening:

> it's already been said.

Hard for them to get used to things like sleep

being gone while we adjust the lights.

SHOPPING IN PORTLAND, OREGON

Cherry blossoms line the Saturday Market
near Burnside. I'm on holiday from hospice work,

except for these ghosts in my luggage,
who thin. Thin again.

I've carried Bob for five years now,
ever since he stopped loading sawed oaks

into his pick-up to fashion roll-top
desks for the Elder Center. His heart gave out.

Not before his wife ignored her headaches until
a clot blocked the gate to her thoughts,

where Bob used to live. No one could forget
that sterile Wednesday by her post-stroke bed,

when she wept and said,
For the love of God, go back. You're dead!

What could he do? Bob slipped off
like the carrots on his wife's weighted spoon

which never could hold much in place.
I head to salvage scavenged bits of nature

which Bob would have given second life.
And, to the cruelty-free shrine beside

the knitted hats that just might keep
us all a bit warmer, listening hard

for the right prayer to lift into this atmosphere,
while the living and the dead watch

ants sprinkle the sidewalks
and bridges build hallways in the sky.

Soon, April. And those of us who'd frozen our fingers clothespinning
children's outfits into brightly colored popsicles, or who'd
shoveled dirty snow just before the town's plow pushed
the icy streets onto our driveways, or who'd spilt the golden
retriever's ashes we'd agreed none of us would scatter
until spring when all of us could gather,
blink away lopsided snowmen blinded by hungry deer. We notice
as the neighbors drag away electric does who've shone
through our windows for so long that our rescue puppy no longer
interrogates them. We cannot help but recall our parent's tree,
its poisoned tinsel, or the year Sheba
swallowed it while large with litter. Or was that
the year she'd widened but didn't whelp, the year
she'd collected and mothered the ornaments,
the year she would not let any of us near the torn rabbit?
Anyway, their deer had stood since before the couple
left to have their daughter, and long after the morning they
returned without her. But let's not fret about Christmas
decorations from our past, or those strewn on our neighbor's
lawn. Mud season arrives despite the stillborn,
the earth rolling over as predicted. If we live long enough,
we pause when the ground softens, the woodpile dampens,
or a sparrow's song is close enough to touch.

ACKNOWLEDGEMENTS

"Dear Grief-Lake" and "Missing" – *Anti-Heroin Chic*

"The Dead" and "In Which I Explain the Signs of Dying"
– *The American Journal of Poetry*

"Rounds" – *Incessant Pipe*

"Shopping in Portland Oregon" – *JAMA*

"The Intersate Spills" – *Pangyrus*

"Sun Ghazal with Burnt Out Shers" – *SWWIM Every Day*

"Kay and Del that First Morning Without Him" and
"Keeping Up Appearances on ABC News March 14th, 1980"
– *The Wax Paper*

"Weather Report" – *Mom Egg Review*

THANK YOU

Thanks to Nixes Mate editors Michael McInnis and Annie Pluto, whose unwavering support made this book possible.Thank you to Dzvinia Or-lowsky and Jennifer Martellli who read this manuscript in earlier drafts and offered their time, talent and guidance. Love and gratitude to the Monday Night Poets and The Wild Geraniums, who read some of these poems in earlier versions.Thanks to poetry tigresses, Cynthia Bargar and Christine Jones. Warm appreciation to Kathleen Aguero and Cate Marvin, for their encouragement, and for writing the blurbs for *Wild Pack of the Living*.

END NOTES

Most of the poems in this collection and especially, Blue-and-White, 1989 KawasakiI Ex-500 Paid for With The $30,000 FROM THE MINI-SERIES I KNOW MY FIRST NAME IS STEVEN are informed by information researched in *I Know My First Name is Steven*, Pinnacle (October 15, 1999) by Mike Echols.

Keeping up Appearances for ABC News March 14th, 1980 is based on the March 14, 1980 Interview with Steven Stayner by ABC News. https://abcnews.go.com/US/video/march-14-1980-interview-steven-stayner-60269400 58

Eileen Cleary is the author of *2 a.m. with Keats* (Nixes Mate, 2021) and *Child Ward of the Commonwealth* (Main Street Rag Press, 2019), which received an honorable mention for the Sheila Margaret Motton Book Prize. She co-edited the anthology *Voices Amidst the Virus* which was the featured text at the 2021 MSU Filmetry Festival. Cleary founded and edits the *Lily Poetry Review* and Lily Poetry Review Books, and curates the Lily Poetry Salon. A multi-Pushcart nominee, her work is published widely in journals and anthologies.

42° 19' 47.9" N 70° 56' 43.9" W

Nixes Mate is a navigational hazard in Boston Harbor used during the colonial period to gibbet and hang pirates and mutineers.

Nixes Mate Books features small-batch artisanal literature, created by writers who use all 26 letters of the alphabet and then some, honing their craft the time-honored way: one line at a time.

nixesmate.pub

Printed in the USA
CPSIA information can be obtained
at www.ICGtesting.com
LVHW090613161124
796751LV00004B/152